Contents

The school trip 2
Sally Ridd

In space 9
Sally Ridd

Skateboard 12
Jean Kenward

Mrs Bolter's car 14
Kathy Henderson

Snow travel 23
Lynne Burgess

Song of the train 26
David McCord

Canals 28
Moira Wood

James in Venice 32
May Smith

The school trip

It was the day of the school trip. The children were going to a railway park to see some old steam engines. When they got to the park, the engine driver let the children see how the steam engine worked.

"Look at the fire in there," said Kamla.

"We have to put lots of coal on the fire to keep it going," said the driver. "The fire makes the water hot, and that makes lots of steam. The steam makes the train go. The steam makes the whistle work, too. Look."

He let Ben blow the whistle. It made everyone jump. Ben liked the driver with his black jacket and leather hat.

"I would like to be a train driver," said Ben.

"Before people had steam engines they used to ride in a horse and cart, like this one," said Miss Hill.

"Look how long the horse's tail is," said Ben.

"What big feet!" said Annie.

"And look at his big bag of hay," said Mark. The driver let the children give the horse some hay to eat.

"Now, if you all get into the cart, we can go for a ride," said the driver. The children jumped into the cart. "Who would like to sit at the front with me?"

"Me!" shouted everyone.

"One at a time!" laughed the driver.

Ben liked the driver's big straw hat.

"I would like to drive a horse and cart," said Ben.

When it was time to go back to school, the children got on to the big blue bus. Ben, Annie and Rob sat at the front.

"This is fun. I can see everything," said Annie. Rob looked down at the cars in the street.

"We are champions of the road up here," he laughed. Ben looked at the bus driver. She had a blue jacket with lots of buttons.

"I would like to be a bus driver," said Ben.

When he got home, Ben told Mum and Dad all about the school trip.

"I've got some little old steam engines," said Dad. "I'll find them and you can play with them."

"I would like that," said Ben. "I'm going to be an engine driver."

Dad soon found the old trains. He helped Ben and Liz to put the tracks out. It took a very long time. At last they started to play with the trains. Suddenly, Digger ran into the room. He ran right into the tracks.

"Watch out!" shouted Ben, but it was too late. The track fell to bits on the floor.

"Oh dear. The trains can't go without a track," said Dad. "I'll have to fix it. Why don't you take Digger out, Ben?"

Ben and Digger went out into the garden to play.

"Never mind, Digger," said Ben. "I don't think I want to be an engine driver after all. I want to drive a horse and cart."

Just then, Kay came by on her horse.

"Oh look!" said Ben. "Hello, Kay. What's your horse called?"

"She's called Dolly," said Kay.

"I would like to have a horse," said Ben. " I would like to drive a horse and cart. I would go for a ride every day and Digger could ride in the cart with me. Digger, come and say hello to Dolly."

Digger came to look at Dolly. Suddenly, Dolly put her head right over the gate to look at Digger. She made Digger jump. Digger was frightened and ran back into the house.

"Well, perhaps not!" laughed Ben. "I didn't know Digger was frightened of horses."

"We have just got time to take Digger for a walk before tea," said Mum. "Come on."

Ben took his go-cart and Mum walked with Digger. In the park they saw Kamla and Ajay playing with their skates and skateboard.

"Look, this is my bus and I'm the champion bus driver," said Ben. Kamla laughed.

"That's not a bus, it's a go-cart," she said. "You are the champion go-cart driver, not the champion bus driver, and I am the champion on a skateboard and Ajay is the champion on skates."

“Let’s have a race to see who is the champion of all,” said Ajay.

“Don’t go too fast,” said Mum. She held on to Digger. So Ben went on his go-cart and Kamla went on her skateboard and Ajay went on his skates and they had a race. Digger wanted to run too. He pulled and pulled until he got away from Mum.

“Look out, everyone,” shouted Mum. “Here comes Digger!” Digger jumped up at the children and they all fell over.

“Oh dear!” laughed Mum. “I think Digger must be the champion at getting in the way!”

In space

We live on a planet called Earth. All around the Earth is air and then there is a big space. In this space are other planets and stars. They are very far away. The moon is the nearest place to the Earth. Some people have been to the moon in a space rocket. These people are called astronauts. It takes about four days to get to the moon in a space rocket.

An astronaut on the moon.

The moon looks like a grey desert with lots of rocks and mountains. People, animals and trees can't live on the moon because there is no air or water. When the astronauts walk on the moon they have to take some air with them. They have to put on a space suit and heavy boots. Without the heavy boots they would float off the moon into space.

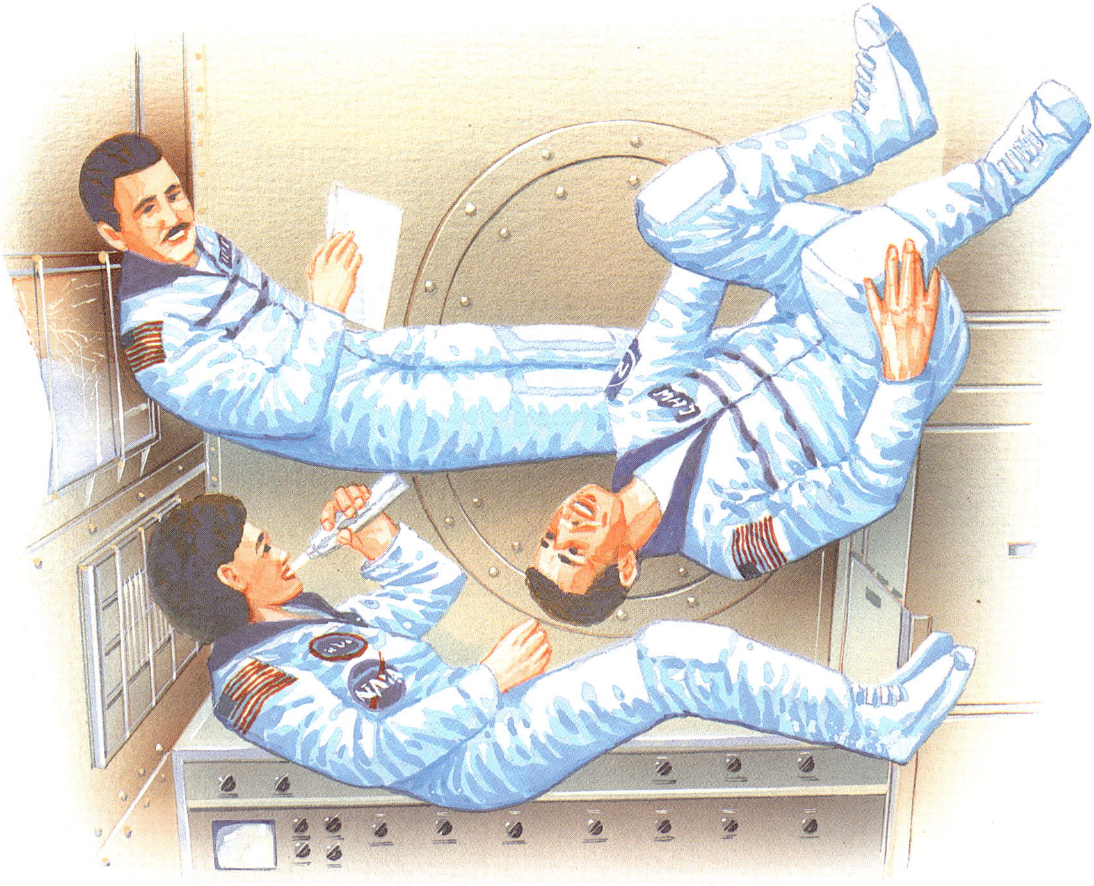

When the rocket is out in space, everything must be tied down because everything floats in space. The astronauts sleep in a bag tied to the wall. They have to suck water through a pipe and eat sticky food that will not float away. If they want to move about in the rocket, they can swim through the air.

When it is time for the astronauts to go home, the rocket comes back to Earth like an aeroplane.

Skateboard

I like to go
from side to side
on a swerving skateboard
feet astride.

I like to swing
this way
and that
wearing a helmet
for a hat.

I like to race
right down our lane,
pick up my board. . .
and start again!

Jean Kenward

Mrs Bolter's car

Mrs Bolter had always wanted a car. Not just any old car but a smart car, a fast car, with shiny wheels and bright red paint and a horn that could be heard all over the city.

The trouble was that Mrs Bolter was poor. She lived in a little grey house in a little grey street in a big grey city. She didn't have a car at all. When Mrs Bolter went anywhere she had to take the bus or walk.

Well, one fine day Mrs Bolter went out walking. The sun was bright. The sky was blue. She came to a rubbish tip. On top of the tip were some wheels. They were old but still shiny.

Mrs Bolter stopped and looked. She looked very hard. And suddenly she thought,

"Why shouldn't I have what I want? I can't afford a smart car but what is to stop me from making one?"

One by one she took the old wheels off the tip and took them home. Then she set to work. Bang! Clang! Clatter! Bang!

Mr Khan came by.

"You look happy," he said. "What are you doing?"

"I'm making a car," said Mrs Bolter. "A smart car, a fast car, with shiny wheels and bright red paint and a horn that can be heard all over the city."

"What a good idea," said Mr Khan. "I think I have just what you need." And off he went. Soon, he came back with a big heavy engine.

"Here you are," said Mr Khan and he set to work too. Bang! Clang! Clatter! Bang!

Ruby Jones came dancing by.

"What are you doing?" she asked.

"We're making a car," said Mrs Bolter, "and not just any car, but a smart car, a fast car, with shiny wheels and bright red paint and a horn that can be heard all over the city."

"That's right," said Mr Khan.

"Oh!" said Ruby. "I think we can help there," and off she went. Soon she came back with her little brother. They were carrying two old car doors. Bang! Clang! Clatter! Bang!

Soon everyone in the street heard that Mrs Bolter was making a car. One by one they brought things for it: lights, some chairs, a floor, a window, a steering wheel, even a carpet. Last to come was old Mr Brown with a big tin of bright red paint and a great big horn.

It was finished at last!

Mrs Bolter stopped working and looked at the car. What a car it was! What a very fine car!

"Let's go for a drive," she said.

So they all got in: Mr Khan, Ruby Jones, old Mr Brown and all the other people from the street. Mrs Bolter took the wheel. She started the engine and off they went, bang, clang, clatter, bang, down the little grey street and out into the big grey city with the horn going all the way.

Everywhere they went people stopped to look.

"What a smart car!" they all said. "What a fast car! What shiny wheels and bright red paint and what a horn!" Mrs Bolter was very proud.

"This is the best car in all the world!" she said.

Bang! Clang! Clatter! Bang!

Snow travel

It is very exciting in the snow. You can play snowballs and make snowmen, but sometimes getting to school can be a problem. If the snow is too deep, the cars get stuck. It feels very strange walking on snow and you soon get tired. Perhaps you could have a ride on a sledge. It feels bumpy but it would be good fun.

The dogs that pull the sledges are called huskies.

Some places don't have much snow but in other places there is deep snow for many months. The people have found new ways to get around. If there are lots of mountains, people sometimes have skis. At first it is hard not to fall over, but even very small children can learn to ski well. Sometimes people have a sledge with dogs to pull them along.

A skiddoo in Canada.

Some people need to go fast through the snow. A sledge is too slow and skis are not so good in flat places. Lots of people ride around on a special machine which can go through snow without any problems. It is called a skiddoo. It goes fast and doesn't mind the ice or deep snow.

Song of the train

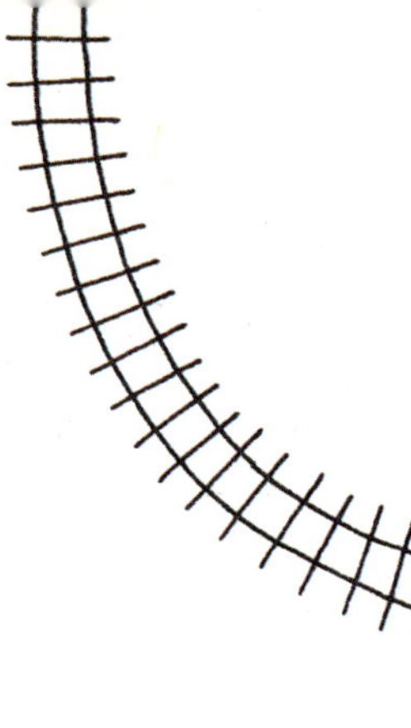

Clickety-clack,
Wheels on the track,
This is the way
They begin the attack:
Click-ety-clack,
Click-ety-clack,
Click-ety, *clack*-ety,
Click-ety
Clack.

Clickety-clack,
Over the crack,
Faster and faster
The song of the track:
Clickety-clack,
Clickety-clack,
Clickety, clackety,
Clackety
Clack.

Riding in front,
Riding in back,
Everyone hears
The song of the track:
Clickety-clack,
Clickety-clack,
Clickety, *clickety*
Clackety
Clack.

David McCord

Canals

A canal family, their horse and their boats, in 1913. The people wore traditional clothes.

Cars go from town to town on a road. Boats can go from town to town on a road of water. A road of water is called a canal.

Many canals were made about two hundred years ago. Horses walked along the path by the canal and pulled big boats with strong ropes. The boats took heavy things from one place to another. They took coal, bricks and even food.

Some boats had beautiful pictures painted on them and every boat had its own name. Sometimes all the family lived and worked on a boat. They had to live in a very small space.

As the water is let out of the lock, the boat goes down to the lower water.

Today, boats have engines, not horses, to make them go. They can go a very long way on the canal, under bridges, over bridges, into tunnels and also through locks. The locks are used to get to higher or lower water. When water is let into the lock, the boat can go up. When water is let out of the lock, the boat can go down. People use a special key to let the water in or out. It's exciting to go through a lock on a boat.

The canal at Little Venice, London.

There are canals in the city as well as in the country. Now they are old and have to be looked after. Many years ago, some canals were not looked after very well so no one could use them for a long time.

Lots of people use canals today. Some like to take a holiday on a canal boat, or go for a day trip on a special boat. Some boats are restaurants where you can go out to eat on the canal. Some people live on house boats on the canal all the time.

Lots of people like to use the canals even if they don't have a boat. Some like to fish in the water. Some go for a walk along the path by the canal. They like to look at the water and trees. They might see animals or birds which live there. If they are very lucky, they might see fish in the water.

James in Venice

There was once a cat called James who ran away to Venice. Venice is a city in Italy, and James found out just what a strange city it is.

It took a long time to get there. First, he went across the sea in a big boat. James didn't like the sea and he didn't feel well on the boat. He was pleased when it was time to get on to the train that went all the way to Italy.

The train went past towns and tunnels and through some very big mountains with snow on top. James looked out of the window until it was night. Then he went to sleep on the floor. When he woke up, he was in Venice.

When James left the station, he had a terrible surprise. There was not one road to be seen! All the streets were full of water, and James didn't like water at all!

"There must have been a lot of rain here," he thought. He started to cross a bridge that went over the street full of water and he stopped a man to ask him about it.

"Has there been a lot of rain?" asked James.

"No," said the man. "Venice is like this all the time. We don't have any roads, just lots of canals. We go about by boat, not by car or bus."

"I don't think I'm going to like it here," thought James. James wanted to see everything, so the man told him to get a water bus. James waited in a bus stop that floated on the water. It moved about and went up and down. James was not at all happy, but then the water bus came and off they went.

James looked at the lovely buildings of the city. They were very old, and they were right next to the canals.

"Venice is a very beautiful city," thought James, "but I don't like all this water."

He got off the bus by a big church. There were lots of people and hundreds of pigeons. Just then, a little grey mouse ran out of the church.

"Get back, everyone!" shouted James. "I'll save you!" He ran after the mouse. It ran near the pigeons and James ran after it. All the pigeons flew up into the air. Birds and feathers went everywhere!

The mouse ran right up to the canal, and James still ran after it. It jumped on to a boat that was moving some chairs to a new house.

"Quick! Jump on here!" shouted a little girl. James looked up. Some children were on their way to school in their family boat. James jumped.

"Come on," cried the little girl. "Let's catch up with the mouse!" Her big brother made the boat go faster and faster, but just as the first boat went under another bridge, the mouse jumped off again. James jumped off too.

The mouse ran along the path by the canal and went over a bridge. It ran on to a big boat which was tied up. This boat was a market stall, and lots of people were doing their shopping. James jumped to catch the mouse, but the mouse was too fast for him. Crash! Everything went flying!

"Hey! Get off my boat!" shouted the woman on the market boat. James tried to run away but then he fell – right into the canal!

"Help me! Help me! I can't swim!" cried James, as he waved a wet paw and splashed about in the cold, green water.

"Hold on to this," called a man and he held out a long pole. James held on to the pole and the man pulled him back to the bank.

"I've never seen a cat that can swim before," said the man.

"I can't swim," said James. "I fell in and now I'm cold and wet. I wanted to see everything, but then I had to save everyone from the mouse."

"You can come with me on my boat," said the man. "You'll soon see everything a better way."

The man was a gondolier. He pushed his long boat along the canals with his big pole.

"My boat is called a gondola," he said. "It's for people to have trips on the canals for fun." He pushed the gondola on and on, under lots of bridges and even under lots of washing. He took James all over Venice and then he got him a big fish to eat. James and the gondolier had lots of fun.

When they had finished eating, James and the gondolier sat by the canal. They could see all the lights of Venice and all the stars in the sky and heard the canal water splashing softly. It was very beautiful.

“I’ve always wanted a cat,” said the gondolier. “I would like you to stay in Venice with me.”

“Then I will stay,” said James. “I like gondolas and I like fish and I like you. I’m not even as frightened of the water as I was. I think I will be very happy here.”